Backyard Cottages & Gazebos

A *Sunset* Outdoor Design Guide

By Josh Garskof and the Editors of *Sunset*

Sunset

©2011 by Time Home Entertainment Inc.
135 West 50th Street, New York, NY 10020

ISBN-13: 978-0-376-01386-6
ISBN-10: 0-376-01386-9
Library of Congress Control Number: 2009941658

10 9 8 7 6 5 4 3 2 1
First Printing January 2011. Printed in the United States of America.

OXMOOR HOUSE
VP, PUBLISHING DIRECTOR: Jim Childs
EDITORIAL DIRECTOR: Susan Payne Dobbs
BRAND MANAGER: Fonda Hitchcock
MANAGING EDITOR: Laurie S. Herr

SUNSET PUBLISHING
PRESIDENT: Barb Newton
VP, EDITOR-IN-CHIEF: Katie Tamony
CREATIVE DIRECTOR: Mia Daminato

Outdoor Design Guide: *Backyard Cottages & Gazebos*
CONTRIBUTORS
AUTHOR: Josh Garskof
MANAGING EDITOR: Bob Doyle
PHOTO EDITOR: Philippine Scali
ART DIRECTOR: Tracy Sunrize Johnson
PRODUCTION SPECIALIST: Linda M. Bouchard
PROOFREADER: John Edmonds
INDEXER: Marjorie Joy
SERIES DESIGN: Susan Scandrett
TECHNICAL ADVISOR: Scott Gibson
COVER PHOTO: Photography by Thomas J. Story

SPECIAL THANKS
The author would like to thank: Les Beckwith (contractor, Wolfboro, N.H., beckwithbuilders.com), Ross Chapin (architect, Langley, Wash., rosschapin.com), Stephanie Curtis (landscape designer, San Jose, Calif., curtishort.com), Roy L. Fyffe (American Association of Code Enforcement), Bud Jenkins (professor of coating science chemistry, California State Polytechnic University, Pomona), Cammie Jones (professional organizer, Seaside, Calif., cjorganizing.com), David Kyle (contractor, Cayuga, Tex., dkyleconstruction.com), Peter Nelson (tree-house builder, Fall City, Wash., treehouseworkshop.com), Alexandra Sheets Saikley (architect, Alameda, Calif., asarch.org), Elida Doldan Schujman (architect, Sausalito, Calif., architecturestudioonline.com), Alan Stein (architect, Denton, Md., tanglewoodconservatories.com). Thanks also to Georgia Dodge, Mark Hawkins, Stephanie Johnson, Laura Martin, Brianne McElhiney, Kimberley Navabpour, Marie Pence, Linda Lamb Peters, Alan Phinney, Amy Quach, Lorraine Reno, Vanessa Speckman, E. Spencer Toy.

To order additional publications, call 1-800-765-6400
For more books to enrich your life, visit **oxmoorhouse.com**
Visit Sunset online at **sunset.com**
For the most comprehensive selection of Sunset books, visit **sunsetbooks.com**
For more exciting home and garden ideas, visit **myhomeideas.com**

IMPORTANT SAFETY WARNING—PLEASE READ

contents

Guesthouses

Whether you're building for overnight company, long-term visitors, or relatives who will move in to stay, a guesthouse that is detached from the main house will maximize their comfort and yours. Guests won't need to worry about disrupting your household, and you won't be so concerned about their privacy.

The consummate guesthouse is a small but complete home in its own right, with a scaled-down version of a master bedroom suite, an efficiency kitchen, and a comfortable place to sit. But this doesn't mean you have to make big commitments of either space or cash, especially if you'll be accommodating mostly short-term visitors. At bare bones, a guesthouse can be little more than a spare bedroom, although a bathroom will make your visitors considerably more comfortable, since they won't have to traipse back and forth to the main house. Be aware, however, that a bathroom ratchets up the cost and complexity because it requires plumbing and, in most climates, insulation and heating.

A sleeping loft with ladder access allows a complete guesthouse to fit into a modest footprint.

Scalloped rake moldings and divided-light windows help to transform a simple garden shed into quaint guest accommodations.

In a small yard, surrounding a guest cottage with garden plants will enhance your visitors' sense of privacy.

We think of roofs as utilitarian necessities, but they can also be sources of cottage charm. Steep peaks provide visual weight, wood shingles add character, and low eaves create human scale.

RIGHT: Situating the guesthouse as close to the property line as possible maximizes the remaining useful backyard space.

FACING PAGE: A single outbuilding can serve multiple purposes, such as a home office upstairs and a guest bedroom downstairs, with a shared bathroom in the back. The rope rails on the stairs wouldn't pass muster with most building codes, however.

choosing the right spot

❯❯ One of the biggest advantages of constructing a guesthouse from scratch is that you get to decide where to put it. In thinking this through, focus not just on the building itself but on how it will affect your yard. "It's easy for homeowners to think about what they want the new building look like, but the space between the buildings is just as important," says Alameda, California, architect Alexandra Sheets Saikley (asarch.org). "Think about the relationship between the buildings and the open space that will remain."

Local building codes typically require
36-inch-high railings—with the open-
ings between their balusters no greater
than 4 inches—around any deck that's
more than 30 inches above ground.

LEFT: The bedroom opens directly into a galley kitchen, minimizing the footprint of the two spaces.

BELOW: Built-in cabinets fill the windowless end wall, eliminating the need for storage furniture along the glass sidewalls.

FACING PAGE: Stacking the kitchen, bedroom, and bathroom in the two-story "tower" means there's no cabinetry, plumbing, or privacy needed in the living room wing. This allows for multiple sliding glass doors leading to the two-tier deck.

DIY cabin

On rough terrain, elevating a building on concrete piers and posts minimizes the site work, environmental impact, and cost of the job.

ABOVE LEFT: Since this rugged guesthouse was designed to be off the grid and is situated a good distance from the main home, a sturdy cooler provides storage for beverages and other essentials.

LEFT: A loft bed, fold-down table, and petite food-prep area are all tucked into one end of the tiny shed.

ABOVE RIGHT: Plywood is an inexpensive, durable, DIY-friendly choice for interior walls. It makes hanging hooks and artwork a snap later on.

private
retreat

A contemporary cabin exploits its private, woodsy location with a large daybed on one deck and an outdoor shower on another.

LEFT: A chalkboard in the galley kitchen lets guests notify their hosts about any dwindling supplies or maintenance issues.

ABOVE: Leaving the roof framing exposed and painting it to match the walls makes the interior feel informal and cozy.

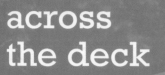

A single-pitch roof focuses the windows toward the deck and swimming pool while dumping snow and rain into the woods.

Cork flooring, plywood walls, and metal loft posts create an upscale country feel that's right at home in the woods.

LEFT: Since only the kitchen and bathroom need plumbing and electricity, they are the only indoor rooms. They are plenty spacious, although the building's footprint is small.

FAR LEFT: The patio of the main house serves as the guests' living room. The sleeping quarters are in an adjacent tent, complete with real mattresses.

design lesson: metal roofing

Long used for barns, metal roofing is an excellent choice for sheds and cabins. It's extremely long lasting and, depending on the materials, can be relatively affordable. Plus, in warm climates its reflective nature helps to repel the sun's heat, while in cold climates it's smooth finish helps to shed snow. The version shown here is a standing-seam roof, which consists of U-shaped strips whose edges are folded over each other and crimped together. This creates a water-tight joint with no exposed fasteners. Such roofing can be fashioned out of anything from affordable galvanized steel panels to pricy zinc or copper.

converted buildings

A rehabilitated barn makes a quirky guesthouse, with circular bedrooms in the old grain silo.

LEFT: Though the car now lives in the driveway, the original garage door remains, allowing the guest suite to become indoor-outdoor space.

BELOW: Exposed framing and carriage house doors provide intriguing architectural character in a guest-house bedroom.

converted garage

The greenest way to build an outbuilding is to reuse the one you already have.

ABOVE: The large front entry, narrow floor plan, and stone paving out front all serve as clues that this Seattle cottage originated as a garage.

FACING PAGE: The one-room living space includes a kitchen along one wall, locker-style closets along the other, and a sleeping loft above.

converted
barn

keep the character of converted buildings

>> An unfinished barn isn't everyone's idea of a welcoming guesthouse, but even if you upgrade an old building into a highly sophisticated space, consider keeping a few hints of the building's history to preserve unique visual interest. Leave a barn's timber framing exposed, for example, or keep a garage's large front openings (even if you fill them with picture windows). And always take plenty of photos of the building in its original state. They'll make fun—and affordable—wall art that pays homage to the structure's past.

LEFT: This farm shed got little more than a good cleaning and a structural check before it was repurposed as the most rustic of guesthouses.

ABOVE: Hand-hewn beams and shabby chic furnishings are part of the charm, making a sleepover feel a little like a brief stay at a dude ranch.

converted trailer

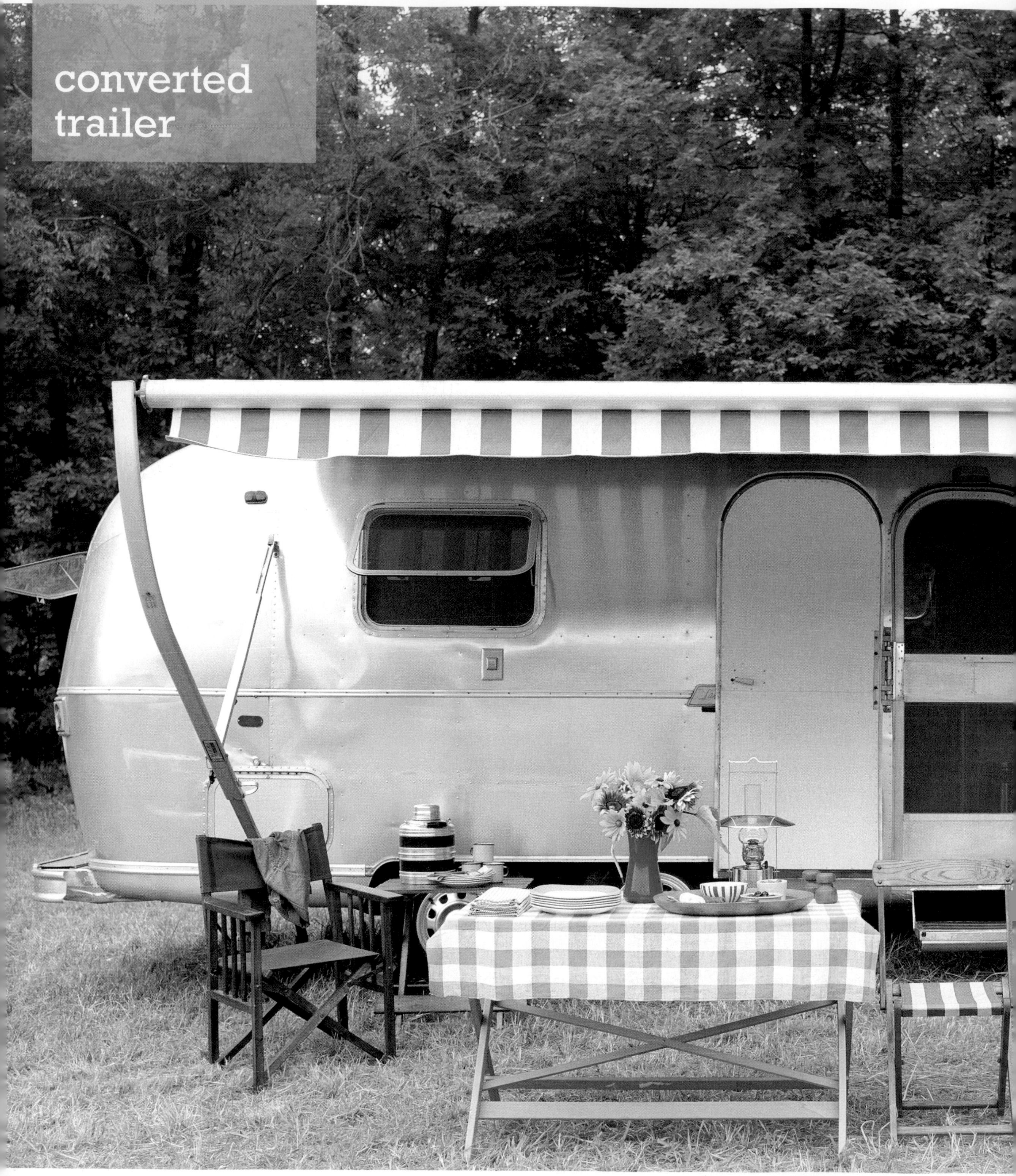

Vintage travel trailers are retro alternatives to contemporary campers and RVs.

LEFT: This 1971 Airstream trailer gets moved to a new spot on its owners' weekend property each year, providing guests a different experience every time they visit.

ABOVE: The galley kitchen—and the whole interior—is designed like a sail boat, with compact appliances and clever storage compartments.

where to put windows

>> You'll want windows where the views are, naturally, but especially when it comes to large expanses of glass, think about their orientation on a compass, says Sausalito architect Elida Doldan Schujman (architecture studioonline.com).

North-facing windows provide pleasing filtered light without adding too much heat to the building.

South-facing windows are also terrific because in the summer, when the sun is high in the sky, they won't bring in much direct sun. Come winter, when the sun is low, your guests will get lots of warming sunshine.

East-facing windows yield nice morning sunshine, which is usually not too hot.

West-facing windows are problematic, says Schujman, because you'll get too much heat from the afternoon sun.

ABOVE: Low-slung windows should be made of tempered glass, which if broken will crumble into harmless cubes instead of shattering into dangerous shards.

FACING PAGE: Since the end—or gable—wall typically doesn't support any roof weight, it can sometimes be replaced entirely with windows.

ABOVE: Eye-level picture windows are unobstructed by mosquito screens or operating hardware, while down below, awning windows provide much-needed ventilation.

FACING PAGE, TOP LEFT: If you're not winterizing the building, there's no need to choose energy-efficient double-paned windows—unless you anticipate adding a heating or cooling system someday.

FACING PAGE, TOP RIGHT: Building codes for windows are based on your climate, with the toughest standards typically found in the coldest regions.

FACING PAGE, BOTTOM: Glass-panel doors fold up accordion-style to create an open air living room.

LEFT: Large sliding glass doors provide natural light, fresh air, and views of the main house, while tiny bedroom and bathroom windows maintain privacy for guests.

RIGHT: A skylight brings daytime illumination—and nighttime star-gazing—to the loft bedroom, without any loss of privacy.

BELOW RIGHT: Looking out the wall of glass, guests can easily see if their hosts have risen and started breakfast.

LEFT: The entire wall of this poolside guesthouse folds upon itself—much like the room dividers in a hotel conference room—so you can keep an eye on swimming kids from your easy chair.

BELOW: In some locations, an open-air guesthouse may require mosquito netting.

FACING PAGE: A stone floor inside and plenty of tall trees outside help to keep a sunny atrium from overheating on a summer day.

FACING PAGE: The simplest guesthouses are one-room sleeping sheds, such as this cabin containing a daybed and surprisingly ornate built-in cabinetry.

RIGHT: A fold-up futon and a shaded outdoor seating area maximize the living space this tiny guesthouse provides.

BELOW RIGHT: Behind one louvered panel, you'll find the bedroom; the other conceals a fold-down desk.

guesthouse interiors

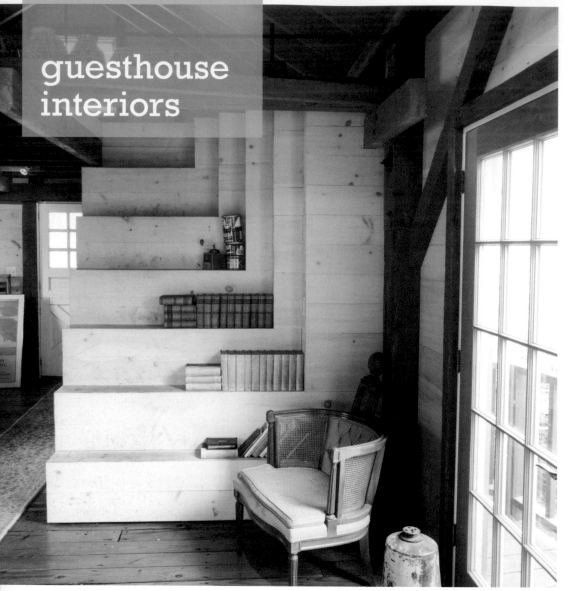

LEFT: Books and collectibles turn the idiosyncrasies of a converted barn into display spaces.

BELOW LEFT: Simple lines, natural materials, and the absence of window moldings and turned furniture legs make this modernist space feel larger.

RIGHT: The structural members in these exposed walls are accented with white trim paint, creating an appealing contrast with the sea-foam blue siding boards.

Open shelving, bare structural framing, and swing-open windows give this guesthouse a cottage feel.

what is cottage style?

» The cottage aesthetic is simple, informal, and colorful, says Langley, Washington, architect Ross Chapin (ross chapin.com) Here are some defining characteristics:

Outside: A rural, naturalistic setting, walls made of boards and battens; steep roof peaks; wide porches; and decorative chimneys.

Inside: Exposed structural members; asymmetrical floor plan; painted wood finishes, beadboard or other paneling; open shelving or hooks; worn surfaces; and an overall feeling of unvarnished country charm.

Just don't overdo the country detailing, Chapin warns. "There's a fine line between a space that feels warm and touchable and something that's overly sentimental," he says. "All it takes are a few small details to create a cottage feel."

BELOW LEFT: In the bathroom, leaving the walls unfinished would expose pipes and vents, so horizontal paneling hides the mess while maintaining the cottage aesthetic.

BELOW: A closet door made from tongue-and-groove paneling wears a drop latch and strap hinges for an authentic early-American look.

The bathroom walls of this modernist guesthouse are constructed much like stairs, with knick-knack shelves for treads and opaque glass for the risers between them.

Whether it's an open cathedral ceiling or the underside of corrugated steel roofing, leaving the underside of the roof exposed adds cottage charm.

To winterize a cottage without giving up the look of exposed walls, a contractor can insulate, then create a faux structural framework over the now weather-tight walls.

LEFT: Folding furniture tucks away when it's not needed, maximizing compact floor space.

ABOVE: A potted plant fills a dead corner, which is too boxed in by other furniture for anyone to use the chair.

Offices and Studios

Put your home office in a freestanding building and you solve the most common problem among the self-employed: too many distractions when they work at home. Whether it'll be a place to handle your primary business, to moonlight after hours, or to tackle a hobby, you'll benefit from getting away from the hustle and bustle of the household. There can even be tax benefits to moving your office or studio into an outbuilding (see page 55).

Depending on your space needs, you could take over an old backyard shed or part of the garage. You could build a small structure from scratch or bring in a prefab one (page 61). In any case, a comfortable workspace usually requires insulated walls and some sort of heating and cooling equipment, such as a space heater and window air conditioner or a built-in system. It also means high ceilings and plenty of operable windows, which will prevent even the tiniest office from feeling claustrophobic. For a music studio, soundproofing will keep your neighbors happy. For a painter's studio, active ventilation will eliminate fumes. And for a home gym or yoga studio, high windows will maintain privacy and provide wall space for large mirrors.

Sometimes you need a change of scenery to keep your creative juices flowing, so this office provides multiple spots to sit and work on a laptop, even outdoors.

FACING PAGE:
Appearing to peel open like a sardine can, this unusual architect-designed office is spacious and bright.

RIGHT: Large windows bring natural light and inspirational garden views into an artist's backyard studio.

ABOVE: A front porch provides an outdoor work space that's protected from sun and rain.

FACING PAGE: A converted potting shed now serves as a Pulitzer Prize–winning journalist's home office in Santa Cruz.

The commute is just seconds long, but you still get separation from nonwork distractions, like to-do lists, telemarketing calls, and those leftovers in the fridge.

one-room office

An office outbuilding needn't be any bigger than the spare bedroom you would otherwise be using in the house.

ABOVE: Double screen doors and a windowed dormer let plenty of fresh air and light into this backyard office.

FACING PAGE: Wallboard and moldings make the office feel finished, even as the exposed rafters keep it airy and informal.

quiet work spaces

LEFT: You don't have to be Henry David Thoreau to see the beauty of a simple workplace that's far away from it all.

ABOVE: An architect's office turns low eaves into an asset, with a wraparound shelf for holding paperwork, books, and knick-knacks.

the tax benefits of a freestanding home office

>> Uncle Sam holds home offices to a looser standard when they're in a shed, garage, or other structure that's separate from the house. Normally, you either have to see clients in your home office or it has to be your principal place of business in order to qualify for a deduction. Not so with a freestanding office. It still must be a dedicated work space, but in general, a home office in an outbuilding doesn't need to be your principal place of work or a place where you see clients in order to qualify. Consult your tax preparer first, but you can generally take the deduction even if it's a secondary work space used only when you don't make you're your usual commute to your employer's building.

studio
interiors

A cable lighting system stretching the length of both eaves allows focused spotlights and diffuse ambient fixtures to be aimed anywhere in the room.

Simple wall-bracket shelving, a vintage school lab chair, and mayonnaise jars recycled as paint containers give this craft space utilitarian good looks.

RIGHT: A vintage draftsman's table makes a practical worktop for an illustrator.

BELOW RIGHT: Original wood floors contrast nicely with this office's sleek and modern furnishings.

Unless you'll be seeing clients there, a home office does not need fancy wood-work or fixtures. Keeping it simple will slash your costs for construction and upkeep.

Exposed timbers lend visual interest—and convenient storage opportunities—in this converted barn.

Modernist lines and
metallic trim aren't
merely style choices;
this shed was made
from a modular kit.

prefab kits

Want a new office without the hassle and wait of building one from scratch? Buy a prefab shed. Home centers and online retailers sell a wide range of standard products that can be retrofitted as a home office. Or you can order one that's specifically designed for the purpose. Sheds like the ones seen here can be ordered online from sites such as studio-shed.com. For between $4,500 and $14,000—depending on the size, materials, and other options you choose—you can buy just about any configuration you want. Kit companies build the shed to your specifications in the factory, then deliver and assemble it, a process that takes not much more than six to eight hours. Or you can choose to assemble it yourself and knock about $400 off the price.

Clearstory and entry windows provide plenty of light yet limit the distraction of backyard activities.

Pool Houses

A pool house can be many things, depending on what fires your imagination. Starting with the basics, it's a place to change and shower without traipsing through the house and, generally, a place to store a collection of water toys and games. But it can also be a backdrop for pool parties with facilities for preparing meals and cocktails by the pool. You could also create a multipurpose pool house that goes well beyond swimming and sunbathing. The building can double as a guest bedroom, a wintertime recreation room, or an indoor party space for off-season gatherings. It can even house a spa, a home gym, or a yoga room.

Whatever you do with it, the pool house should enhance the appeal of your property. Adding a small outbuilding that harmonizes with the architecture of your home and your pool's environs will bring a visual focal point to the landscape. It will hide the pump, heater and other pool equipment, which can be tucked away inside the building. And it can turn your whole yard into something much more practical, convenient, and beautiful.

This pool house enhances nighttime swims by providing warm indoor showers and ambient light.

FACING PAGE: An ivy-covered arbor and fieldstone walls give this pool a natural flavor, almost as if you've come upon a lake in the woods.

RIGHT: An upscale outhouse—complete with mosaic tiles and a vessel sink—means nobody has to track wet feet through the house to use the facilities.

BELOW: The wall down the center of this pool house separates the private shower and bathroom in the back from the open poolside seating area in front.

ABOVE: The showers are at one end of this clever structure, a wet bar is at the other end, and cozy all-weather furniture occupies the middle, with a retractable awning to shade the late-afternoon sun.

FACING PAGE: Even a pool house that holds nothing more than the pump, heater, and cleaning tools can create a beautiful backdrop to the water.

pool house options

What features will you put in your pool house? Here are 10 to consider:

» A utility room to hide your pump and pool-cleaning tools.

» A restroom with a nonslip tile floor.

» An indoor or outdoor shower connected to a hot-water supply.

» A seating area with waterproof furniture and shade.

» A storage area for floats, toys, and other gear.

» A dining area, indoor or outdoor, for serving snacks and meals.

» A wet bar for serving everything from chilled chardonnay to blended tropical drinks.

» A simple kitchen, indoors or out, for preparing poolside barbecues or perhaps even more elaborate meals.

» A ceiling fan to keep people cool on hot afternoons.

» A fireplace to keep everyone toasty after the sun goes down.

Security fencing is a must for an in-ground pool, but it needn't be tight against the water. If possible, keep your patio and pool house inside the fence line.

ABOVE: Even a simple prefab shed can hide the pool equipment and provide storage for pool and patio gear.

FACING PAGE: A large rear window keeps this pool house from completely obstructing the view of the property beyond it, and a vented cupola helps to keep the seating area cool.

open-air pool houses

ABOVE: A house of stone inspired this poolside shade structure, where a couple of large beams are the only non-masonry materials.

FACING PAGE: Here, the construction is all wood, highlighted by a diving platform that releases a waterfall into the pool.

ABOVE: When an open-air kitchen shed proved too small for both cooking and eating, a simple wooden arbor expanded the shady entertaining space.

RIGHT: A cross between a tropical palapa and a diving platform, this pool house couldn't be closer to the water unless it were floating.

Pool houses aren't just for swimming pools; this relaxing spot sits adjacent to a reflecting pool.

Bamboo shades and
latticework lend a
feeling of enclosure
to an open-air room
that's close enough
to please a lifeguard.

ABOVE: The ultimate pool house is a large entertaining space that just happens to double as a poolside patio.

FACING PAGE TOP: Accordion-style doors fold away to create an indoor-outdoor space with views of the pool and beyond.

FACING PAGE BOTTOM: This kitchen and dining area contains a fireplace that extends the usable season far beyond the best swimming weather.

LEFT: Despite its petite size, this pool house manages to provide a wet bar, bathroom, shower, and even a cozy reading loft.

FAR LEFT: A Dutch door encourages guests to stay put by the pool while the hosts prepare a round of snacks and drinks.

Stone tiles make elegant pool-house floors. They are impervious to water and textured enough to provide secure footing even when wet.

ABOVE: A wooden stall is the simplest form of outdoor shower, and no drain is necessary, thanks to a bed of sand covered by spaced decking.

FACING PAGE: Slatted siding on a shower shed provides some degree of privacy while also allowing plenty of ventilation to prevent mold growth.

On-demand water heaters make hot water only when the shower is running, so operating costs are low.

bathhouse
retreat

LEFT: There's no more comfortable place to soak than in a large, deep claw-foot tub. Here the outer shell was dressed up with gray-green paint.

BELOW LEFT: An upholstered chair might seem an odd choice for a bathhouse, but it's a water-resistant fabric.

FACING PAGE: The Boston ivy growing on this converted garden shed changes with the seasons: soft green in spring, vivid red in fall, and rich brown in winter.

ABOVE: A sun-warmed barrel of water supplies this simple curtain-walled shower.

FACING PAGE: A stall constructed of 1-by-6 decking boards and fed by the water system of the main house creates a quick and inexpensive shower room.

privacy options for outdoor showers

You don't have to build walls around your shower to give your family and friends privacy. Here's a sampling of other options:

Halo curtain A circular rod hung above the shower allows the bather to pull a curtain around the entire perimeter.

Fencing Set posts and hang sections of home center fencing to create a private shower stall.

Living screen A few well-placed shrubs with thick foliage can block sight lines to the shower area.

Glass doors Opaque glass panels offer a sophisticated visual barrier.

Faux bamboo shades A simple roll-down shade may be all you need, but choose a waterproof faux bamboo to avoid rot.

pool house interiors

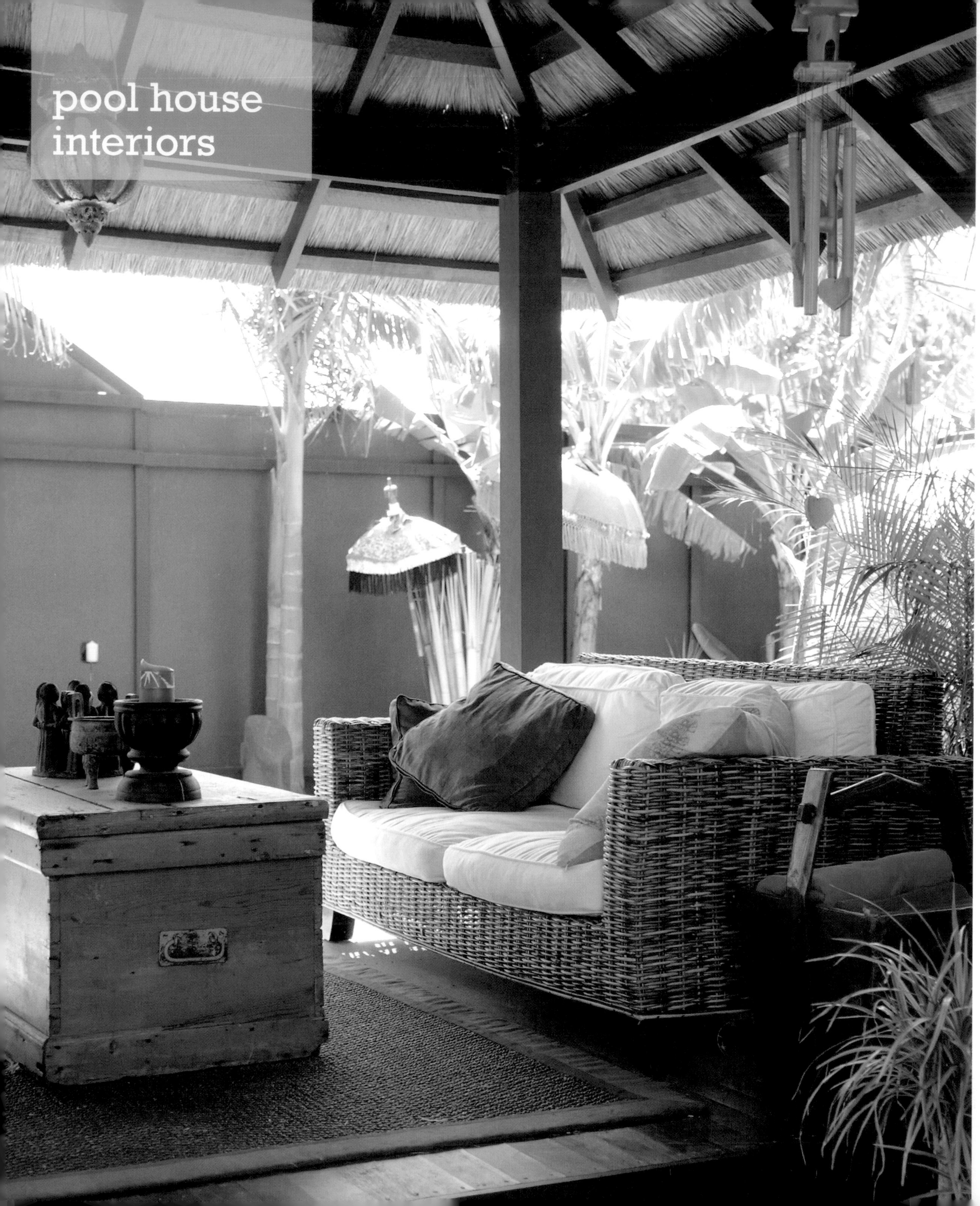

FACING PAGE: You can get the look of natural sea-grass carpeting and wicker from furniture made of weather-proof plastics.

BELOW: A simple bench-style window seat turns a little extra room on the side of a pool utility shed into a cozy waterside seating area.

BELOW RIGHT: Floor-to-ceiling curtains offer respite from the late-afternoon sun. They also create a private changing spot in the corner of the room.

Direct sunshine is welcome while you are in the pool, but after you've dried off, a pool house offers some much-needed shade.

Boathouses

You don't have to own an antique wooden vessel or a sleek catamaran to need a boathouse. Even personal watercraft, kayaks, and dinghies require safe stowing. To provide protection for whatever equipment you own, boathouses come in three basic forms: a roof above a dockside mooring, a water-bottomed garage, or a shed set a few yards onshore with some means for hauling the boat inside.

Still, for many waterfront dwellers, a boathouse is less about nautical needs than providing a cozy hangout by the shore. They think of their boathouses in much the same way other people think of pool houses: as graceful spots for entertaining by the water.

Nowadays, local governments—and other regulators—strictly control waterfront construction (see page 93), so adding a boathouse can get complicated. The exception is with certain existing structures that predate the newer regulations and thus are grandfathered or exempted from current rules, even as you renovate the buildings to suit your needs.

Lightweight canoes are easy to carry across the dock and compact enough to leave plenty of space inside the shed for fishing gear, barbecue provisions, and other lakeside supplies.

living
spaces

This boathouse is also a full-scale vacation home with its own dock, so visitors can come by land or by sea.

ABOVE: An attached garage doubles as a boathouse for a family's light-weight craft.

FACING PAGE: It's a boathouse during the off-season, but when its vessel is on the water, patio furniture turns the interior into a peaceful retreat.

Just as with a garage, the importance of having a boathouse increases proportionally with the value of the vehicle.

building by the water

Of all the projects described in this book, none are so tightly regulated as boathouses—and for good reason. Officials need to protect fragile wetland ecosystems and local drinking water supplies. Moreover, they strive to prevent projects that could exacerbate beach erosion or flooding.

The rules differ from one body of water to the next, but here are some common restrictions, courtesy of two boathouse contractors, Les Beckwith, of Lake Winnipesaukee, New Hampshire (beckwithbuilders.com), and David Kyle, of Richland

Chambers Lake, Texas (dkyle construction.com):

» No living spaces or plumbing within 50 feet, or some other locally specified setback, from the water.

» No solid walls over the water (to prevent people from covertly turning their boathouses into living spaces).

» Building must accommodate specific site issues, including sand characteristics and "fetch" (the prevailing direction of currents and waves).

Even a small dockside shed can stow fishing and recreational gear along with a canoe or two.

A retired boathouse now serves as a changing room for swimmers.

LEFT: Elevating a structure protects it from inevitable floods so it will last for generations.

BELOW LEFT: A fixed-dock gazebo welcomes visitors arriving from across the lake.

You don't have to own a boat to find lots of enjoyable uses for an old waterside building.

In the warmest U.S. climates, you may be able to safely store your watercraft in a boathouse year-round.

LEFT: Even though their hulls are waterproof, the topsides of wooden boats need shelter from the weather.

FACING PAGE: Just as if you were parking in a garage, you steer your boat inside to park it. However, many boathouses contain lifts to pull the craft out of the water for protection.

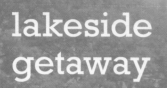

lakeside getaway

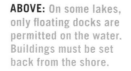

ABOVE: On some lakes, only floating docks are permitted on the water. Buildings must be set back from the shore.

FACING PAGE, TOP: Local codes dictate how high your building must be elevated based on the topography of the area.

FACING PAGE, BOTTOM: The simplest waterside rooms have no plumbing or heating systems, just a woodstove to warm things up on demand.

Party Sheds

A party shed is like the back porch, dining area and family room all rolled into one. It's a place to host small family events and larger get-togethers for neighbors and friends. For some folks living in smaller homes, it's the auxiliary entertaining space that couldn't be squeezed into the main house.

As you'll see on the pages that follow, there are no rules whatsoever about what people do with party sheds. The buildings range from tiny wet-bar huts to small freestanding porches to cabin kitchens equipped to turn out meals on tables scattered around an adjacent patio. Some combine built-in barbecues and sheltered dining halls. Others are under-the-gazebo family rooms with dedicated fire pits and hot tubs.

You can create a party shed from scratch or adapt one from almost any existing outbuilding. Empty a garden shed and give it a coat of paint, and it may serve as a quirky bar space for backyard parties. Clear out the garage, and you've got the room you need for a dance floor. In fact, a party shed doesn't necessarily have to be a structure at all. A patio situated under a leafy canopy of trees may be just the place for summer gatherings.

An underground electrical supply provides power for lights to dine by after dark—and for the bartender's blender.

Who says the outdoor kitchen has to be outdoors? A shed enclosure expands your options for kitchen components beyond weatherproof materials.

ABOVE: A small kitchen shed serves a court-yard eating area.

FACING PAGE: For parties, the band sets up inside and the dancing spills onto the deck.

If your home doesn't comfortably accommodate large gatherings, it may be simpler to transform the yard than to enlarge the house.

ABOVE: A concealed patio on an urban lot puts a fireplace and cozy cushioned furniture out of the public eye.

FACING PAGE: Thanks to the wind-chill factor, ceiling fans cool you down by as much as 8 degrees while using less electricity than a light bulb.

If you've hired someone to do the upkeep on your yard, you may not need that tool shed anymore. With some cleaning and painting, you've got a comfortable new spot for relaxation.

LEFT: Bifold doors allow this porch in a box to open fully onto the yard.

ABOVE: A converted tool shed has become a favored backyard sitting room.

open-air party rooms

The fireplace in this elaborate dining gazebo has a steel guillotine cover to keep out moisture and animals when it's not in use.

zoning rules for outbuildings

» It's your property, but there are rules about what you can build and where. Though local zoning laws differ widely, here are some things you may encounter, according to Roy L. Fyffe, a building official in Burnet, Texas, and spokesman for the American Association of Code Enforcement.

Setbacks In residential areas, you're generally not allowed to build anything within 20 feet of the front of your property, 7½ feet of either side, or 15 feet of the rear.

Coverage limits The portion of your property that can be covered with impermeable materials (including both structures and paving) may be limited to anywhere from 25 to 75 percent of the lot.

Wetlands If your property contains a wetland—or abuts one—your ability to build may be restricted by laws intended to protect aquatic wildlife.

Accessory dwelling restrictions Many towns ban or severely limit any outbuildings designed as dwellings.

Covenants and deeds Some subdivision rules ban outbuildings completely, while others demand extra-large setbacks.

A hot tub and fire-place mean you can use your party space year-round.

A "roof" of leafy tree limbs provides dense cover for a paved outdoor party space.

A simple canvas canopy provides a shady dining space anytime you need one.

Playhouses and Tree Houses

Even in an age of video games, smart phones and short attention spans, a backyard playhouse will keep a lot of kids out in the fresh air until you call them in for dinner. Few other gifts you can give them—apart from high-maintenance options such as a dog or a swimming pool—are likely to be so cherished and become so ingrained in their memories.

To create something fully engaging, give the building fun but simple details, such as windows, kid-size furniture, and a colorful paint job. Girls may tend to use it to play house, while boys may prefer to call it a fort. But it's a good idea to follow their leads, to the extent that you can, in choosing features that inspire a wide range of role-playing games.

By age 8 or 9, children may start to lose interest in a ground-level building. And that's when a little altitude goes a long way. There's something so thrilling about a tree house that even "tweens" tend to stay interested, although they may begin spending some of their time in such a hideaway doing homework or sending text messages.

If a grownup can't fit easily through the front door, kids feel like they've got a place of their own.

gallery of playhouses

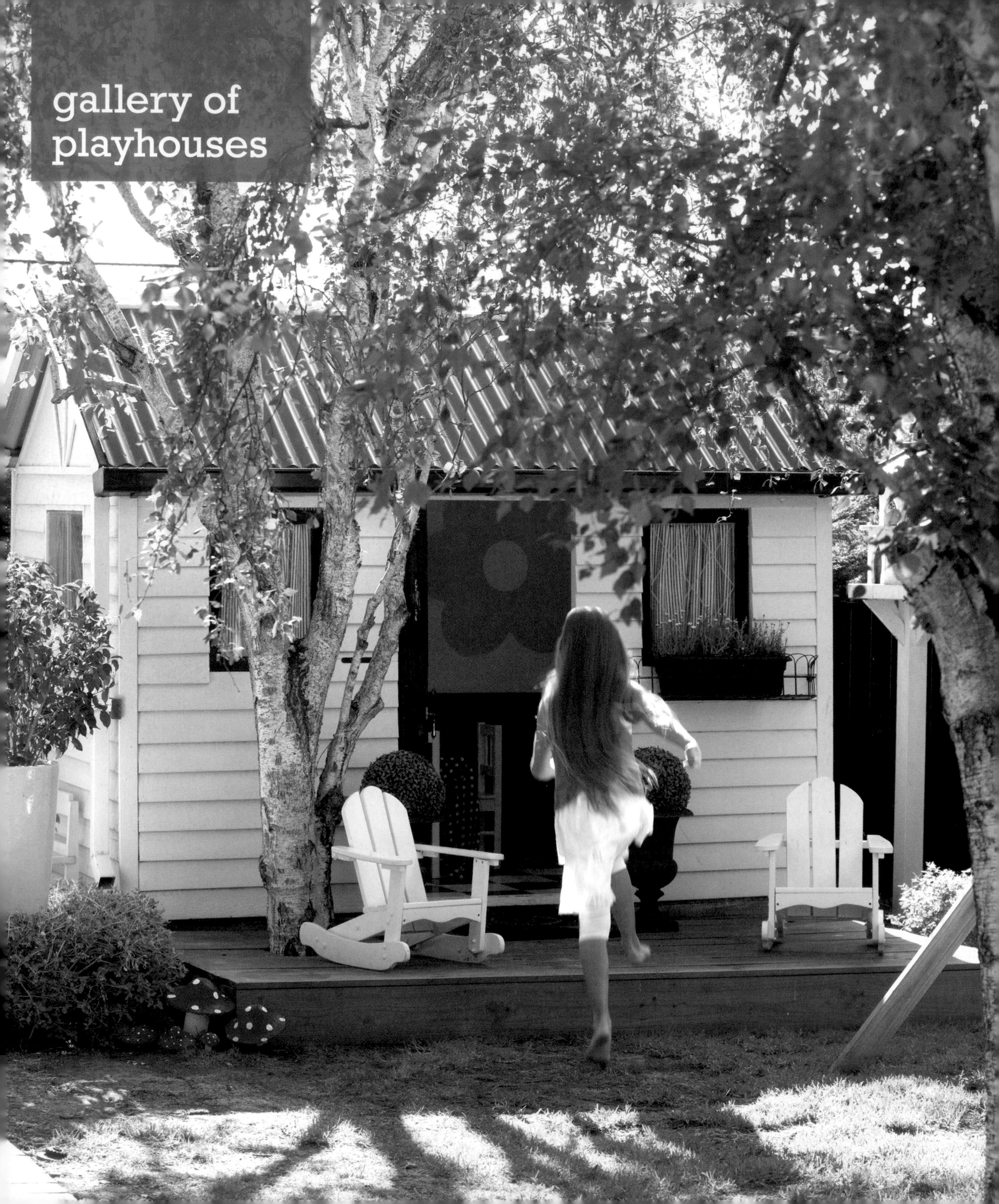

LEFT: Raising a playhouse on piers means you don't have to worry about sloped terrain.

ABOVE: Let the kids take ownership of the house, helping to paint colorful highlights, for instance, or plant sunflower seeds in the spring.

FACING PAGE: All you need to turn a basic backyard shed into an exciting play space are some brightly colored trimwork and kid-size furniture.

RIGHT: Acrylic panes have the feel of real windows without the hazard of breakable glass.

FACING PAGE: As long as it's weatherproof, a playhouse can serve as the kids' primary playroom, loaded with their favorite toys, games, and craft supplies.

gallery of tree houses

Limbs in trees that lose their leaves each fall, such as oaks and maples, are stronger than limbs of the same diameter in evergreens, such as redwoods, pines, or cedars.

ABOVE LEFT: Nestled into a seven-stemmed maple, this Oregon structure was built for adults but was quickly annexed by the kids.

LEFT: It's far simpler to build a fort on man-made stilts than to attach it to live branches.

ABOVE: This 400-square-foot guesthouse has no plumbing, but it does have electrical service and a wraparound deck overlooking a pond.

ABOVE: For kids, the only thing better than having a building of their own is having one that's high in the air.

RIGHT: This playhouse has no perforations for branches. It's a self-contained shed that just happens to live in the embrace of a few hefty limbs.

FACING PAGE: Trees pierce the floors, decks, and even roof of this nautically inspired fort.

Before building in any tree, have
it inspected by a licensed arborist.
You can find one at isa-arbor.com.

live-tree construction techniques

Here are some dos and don'ts from master tree-house builder Peter Nelson, of Fall City, Washington (treehouseworkshop.com): **Don't** put nails or screws into the tree. **Do** use through-bolts in predrilled holes, with washers and nuts on their ends. **Don't** space bolts closer than 12 inches, or the tree may treat both holes as a single wound, leading to bolt-loosening rot. **Do** align holes vertically when possible to reduce the damage to the tree's nutrient flow.

Don't build a tree house without accounting for the swaying of limbs in the wind. **Do** use slider hardware (available at treehouse workshop.com) to allow movement between the tree house and trees. **Don't** allow the tree house to touch the tree, or it can cause friction burns. **Do** rest the tree house on the slider hardware. **Don't** trim bark or wood to create flat mounting areas for tree house parts. **Do** fasten custom-cut wood blocks to the tree house, allowing the attachment hardware to accommodate the tree's natural form.

ABOVE: Thanks to a steep ridge, this high-altitude tree house is accessible via a rope bridge that is a bit of an adventure in itself—and clearly not one for small children.

FACING PAGE: Even the most substantial tree house may intimidate some potential visitors if getting inside requires climbing a ladder. To interest adults—or very young children—you'll want stairs.

Fashion designer Todd Oldham's Pennsylvania tree house offers sweeping views of the valley below and invites serenades from songbirds just outside the windows.

LEFT: Bunk bed railings made from found branches provide a visceral connection between the building and its environment.

BELOW LEFT: Built-in cabinetry is a great way to stow late-night party supplies, such as cocktail glasses, board games, and a few 1950s B movies.

Hiring a high-end specialty firm to design and build a custom kids' tree house typically costs anywhere between $7,000 and $30,000, depending on size, height, design complexity, and materials.

Arbors and Gazebos

Though they're among the simplest projects in this book, shade structures can completely transform any backyard. Adding one to your property will expand your living space "outside the box" of your house's walls. It will turn even a sun-baked patch of land into a comfortable oasis, add visual interest to the landscape, and increase your property's value.

You'll see dozens of fantastic examples on the following pages, loosely grouped into two categories: Arbors don't have solid roofs; they either create only partial shade or have a symbiotic relationship with a stand of wisteria or other flowering vine that provides the solar screening. Gazebos, on the other hand, do have sun-blocking roofs and usually floors and railings too.

Whatever type of shade structure you choose, making it harmonize with your home requires letting the main building's identifying characteristics guide your design choices. Whether it's traditional or contemporary, ornate or simple, stucco or clapboard, painted or stained, stay with the same themes to create something that truly belongs. After all, if you use rot-resistant wood, such as redwood, cedar or mahogany, your creation will last a lifetime.

There's more to gazebos than just providing a sheltered spot to relax. This colorful structure creates an architectural focal point in a garden.

Lattice is normally used vertically, for fencing or screening, but here it's laid horizontally over an ivy-less arbor to moderate the midday sunshine.

Dappled sunlight keeps the picnic table bright, cheery, and mildew-free—without overheating guests.

ABOVE: The best way to prolong the life of your arbor is to apply the paint, or whatever finish you're using, on all six sides of each piece of wood—after they're cut to size but before they're assembled.

FACING PAGE: Space the crossbars of your arbor wide enough apart that you can fit between them to prune and tend the vines from a stepladder down below.

LEFT: Blooming wisteria offers more than a visual delight. Your entire yard will fill with its amazing fragrance.

FACING PAGE: An unusual tunnel-like trellis made of dowels threaded through a 4 x 4 framework makes guests feel like they're dining in a cave of foliage.

great shade plants

Most arbors don't provide much shade on their own. It's the climbing plants that act as the sunscreens. So what should you plant on your arbor? The best choices lose their leaves for wintertime, says Stephanie Curtis, a San Jose landscape designer and contractor (curtishort.com).

"That allows the arbor and the patio underneath to get some sun in the off-season, warding off mold and rot," she says. "Plus it makes it easier to do maintenance pruning if there's no foliage in the way." Her favorite choices are wisterias, grapes, and kiwis.

fabric-covered arbors

LEFT: Man-made acrylic fabrics (such as the Sunbrella and Perennials brands) mimic the look of traditional canvas, but they resist water, mildew, and stains—and last far longer than natural materials.

FACING PAGE: A temporary awning will provide cover for a few years until the vine becomes thick enough to block the midday sun.

ABOVE: The classic gazebo is a six- or eight-sided building with porch-style railings on all but one side. You can buy factory-built models, as well as construction plans or precut kits to assemble yourself.

FACING PAGE: Your gazebo will be a favorite hangout spot even after the sun goes down. Here, candles and tiki torches illuminate a romantic dinner for two.

ABOVE: Windows, doors, and solid walls mean you can enjoy your gazebo in all kinds of weather—and outfit it with built-in cabinets and furniture.

FACING PAGE: A roof-top shade structure screens out more than just the sun; it improves the family's outdoor privacy too.

You generally don't need to get
a building permit for a gazebo
or arbor, unless it's going to be a
whopping 200 square feet or larger.

Traditionally, gazebos are placed to take advantage of the most beautiful views, and they're given eye-catching features of their own to return the favor.

LEFT: Pointed arches, floral tapestries, and on-the-floor seating give this gazebo Asian flair.

FACING PAGE: A tapered roof and decorative window mullions give an otherwise boxy building distinctive cottage style.

145

This Los Angeles poolside structure is made from common gazebo materials—concrete and wood—but reversed. The sculpture-like concrete building shades a wood patio.

Gazebos are especially handy by the water's edge, as they block ultraviolet light better than any sunscreen.

ABOVE: Chaise lounges are expected under a gazebo, but hammocks dangling over a wading pool are not.

FACING PAGE: On a stair-landing gazebo, you can stage swimming and fishing gear before you descend to the water.

ABOVE: The stuff of working barns and tool sheds, corrugated steel roofing is also right at home with sophisticated gazebo designs.

FACING PAGE: Broad arches add a striking visual element to an otherwise straightforward gabled building.

ABOVE: A freestanding screened room expands the usable space at a tiny weekend cabin in the Catskill Mountains of New York.

FACING PAGE: Floor-to-ceiling screens provide unencumbered views of a nearby lake, while wooden privacy panels impede views to and from the abutting property.

The solid interior wall is structurally unnecessary, but it provides a sense of solidity that makes this screened-porch-without-a-house feel rooted to its spot. Plus, it provides a place to hang artwork

You can make nearly any arbor or gazebo bug-free with a screening kit, available at home centers and from online merchants.

Greenhouses

Does your gardening season fly by too fast each year? A greenhouse will change that. Before the last frost has melted, you'll already be tending the seedlings that will become your vegetable and flower gardens. And long after the summer has gone, you'll still be picking salad greens and grape tomatoes from your indoor garden.

You can also use your hothouse to grow tropical plants that normally wouldn't survive in your climate, from citrus trees to orchids and bromeliads. But in areas with cold winters, that requires a greenhouse with electricity, heat, and an insulated foundation. Those features up the project costs significantly, so the vast majority of hobbyist greenhouses in the northern tier of the country are used for three seasons only.

The simplest way to get a greenhouse is to buy a kit, and they come in a huge array of styles, sizes, and materials. You can spend less than $1,000 for a small portable aluminum frame covered with plastic sheeting—or from $2,000 to $8,000 for a substantial building with glass panes. A custom-built greenhouse, of course, can run several times that much.

A stone knee wall, a pediment entrance-way, and ornamental ridge cresting give a cottage-like feel to a house of glass.

gallery of greenhouses

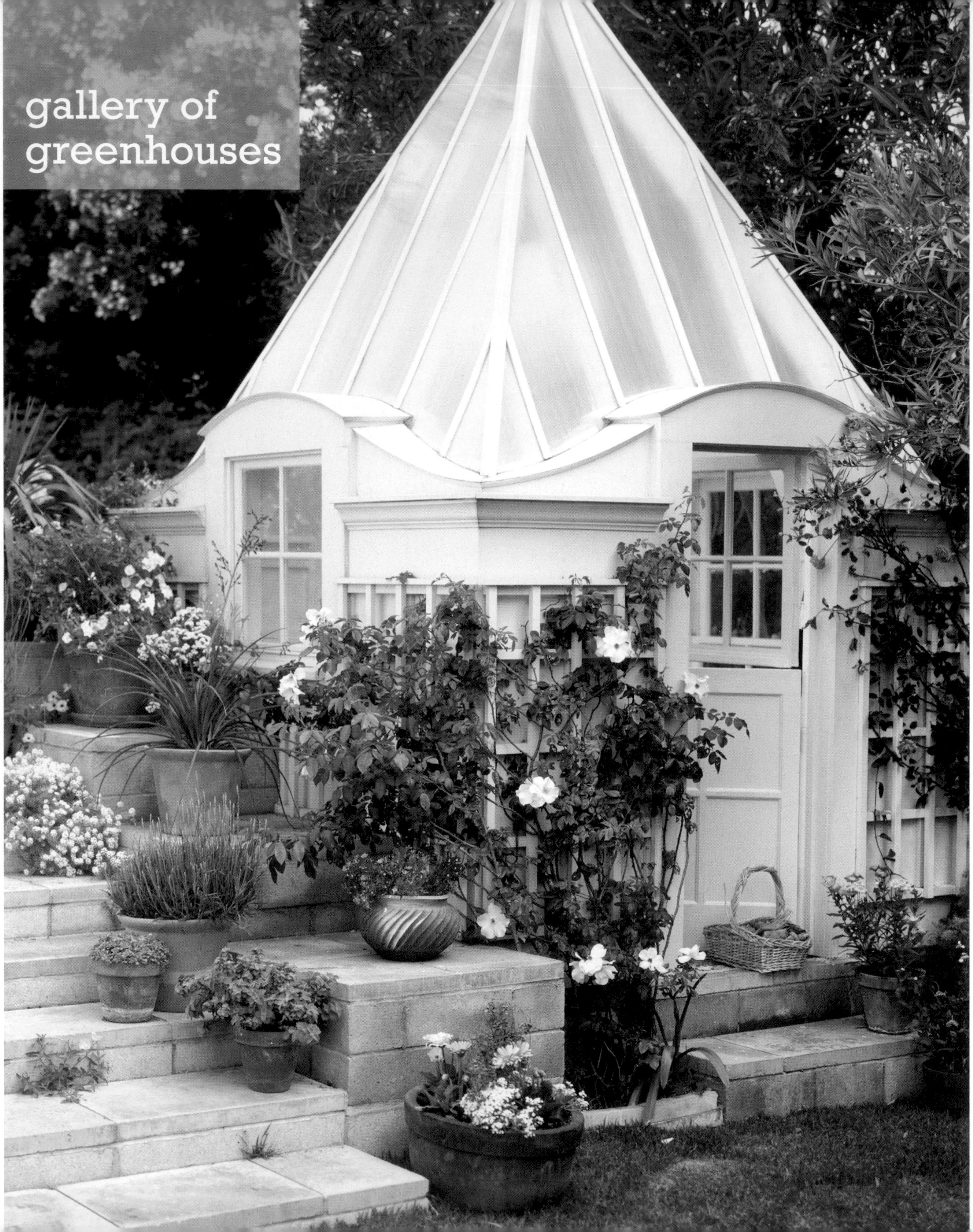

ABOVE: Greenhouses work by admitting solar radiation in through the glass and then trapping the resulting heat inside—much like what happens in a car that's been parked in the sun.

FACING PAGE: Replacing the old asphalt shingles with a clear plastic roof turned this garden shed into a grow house.

With a potting shed and greenhouse joined at the hip, you won't have to do your planting and potting in the tropical heat.

Like a fish tank, a greenhouse should contain compatible elements. Some plants need cold nights, for example, while others need warmth around the clock.

Many homeowners prefer the look of glass to plastic alternatives for their hothouses, but if you live where the ground freezes, a glass greenhouse must sit on a full-fledged foundation or frost heaves will break the panes.

ABOVE: During the hottest weeks of the summer, your greenhouse may not get much use when everything is flourishing outside. But come fall, you can grow a second round of spring veggies inside.

FACING PAGE: A two-story-high greenhouse like this isn't a great choice in cold climates, because you need to be able to brush snow off the roof to protect the glass and allow sunshine inside the building.

ABOVE: Most kit greenhouses have this distinctive barn-roof shape, which makes them strong, easy to assemble, and good at shedding rain and snow.

FACING PAGE: With some modular greenhouses, you can order as many linear sections as you want and plunk the assembly directly on an existing backyard patio.

LEFT: Paving stones create an indoor patio, while the rest of the greenhouse has a gravel floor to quickly drain away moisture.

FACING PAGE: Greenhouse gardening requires careful temperature control. In summer, you'll need lots of ventilation to avoid overheating plants. In winter, you may need a heater.

ABOVE: Sun-blocking shades, ceiling fans, and plenty of high windows make a converted greenhouse livable on mild days, but air conditioning is a must for true summer comfort.

FACING PAGE: Leaving the large doors open keeps this dining space from overheating on a spring day.

heating a conservatory

» In many areas, a greenhouse used as living space—known as a conservatory—needs not only air conditioning but also heat. And the best way to deliver it is with a forced-air system, says Denton, Maryland, architect Alan Stein (tanglewoodconservatories.com). "Forced air delivers heat quicker than other options, such as radiant floors," he says. "More importantly, it also shuts down faster, which is crucial because when the sun comes up in the morning—or breaks through the cloud cover—things warm up fast in an all-glass building."

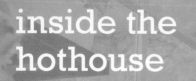

inside the
hothouse

A stone floor helps to keep a greenhouse work area from getting unbearably hot, especially if you do your potting in bare feet.

ABOVE: Within any greenhouse there are microclimates—warm, sunny spots and cooler, shadier spots. Once you figure them out, you can determine which plants belong in which locations.

ABOVE RIGHT: A shelf of hanging sun-lovers helps to shade and protect the low-light varieties growing on the countertop below.

To manage the temperature in your greenhouse, you will adjust a series of high and low vents, creating a chimney effect that exhausts rising hot air at the top and draws in cooler air down below.

Utility Sheds

Why do you want a backyard shed? Perhaps you need a better parking spot for your riding mower, a place to pot plants and start seeds, a full-fledged carpentry workshop, storage for mountain bikes and other recreational gear, or a convenient place to stow outdoor furniture and lawn games for the off-season.

The stuff you'll put in your shed says a lot about who you are, and it should also inform the design of the building. A potting shed, for example, might have a gravel floor to easily accommodate spills. A wood shop needs lots of open space, bright lights, and heavy-duty wiring to run the power tools. And if you'll be using the structure to store anything on wheels, from a snowblower to a motor scooter, you'll want a floor that's flush with the outside terrain—or at least close.

Whatever the purpose, your building project is also a great opportunity to add charm to the backyard. A few simple details—like divided-light windows, plank siding, or decorative moldings—will dress up even the simplest box shed and improve not just the way you use your property but also its beauty.

When the homeowner replaced her house's windows, she installed some of the old ones in her new potting shed for seed-starting purposes. But don't add so much glass to your building unless you're prepared to keep it neat and presentable inside at all times.

Double doors create
a generous opening
that helps get bulky
tools, supplies, and
equipment in and out
of your shed.

ABOVE: There are two keys to great flower boxes: Always pitch them away from the building (to avoid water damage) and fertilize them every couple of weeks (because there's a limited nutrient supply in such a small amount of soil).

choosing exterior finishes

» Unless you're using a rot-resistant wood, such as redwood, teak, or mahogany, your outdoor structure needs protection from the elements. Here's how to assess the options, from Bud Jenkins, professor of coating science chemistry at California State Polytechnic University, Pomona.

Paint Because it forms a hard shell over the wood, paint creates the toughest shield against both moisture, which causes rot, and ultraviolet light, which degrades wood fibers. The downside, though, is that when it's time to repaint, you'll first need to scrape away any loose finish.
ESTIMATED LIFE OF FINISH: 5–10 years

Opaque stain With the same range of colors as paint, and a finish that looks almost identical to it, you get nearly the same level of water and UV protection in a product that soaks into the wood and therefore generally doesn't need scraping before you refinish.
ESTIMATED LIFE OF FINISH: 5–10 years

Semitransparent stain These traditional stains come in a range of browns, reds, and yellows. Whatever the color, the darker the better, says Jenkins, because it's the pigments that block the UV rays. No scraping needed to refinish.
ESTIMATED LIFE OF FINISH: 1–3 years

Clear sealer These go on invisibly, maintaining a natural wood look, while adding water repellency, mold resistance, and UV protection. Look for a product that contains at least 1 percent UV inhibitors and lists two ingredients, HALS/UVA (hindered amine light stabilizers and ultraviolet absorbers) on the label. No scraping needed, but you'll need to reapply frequently.
ESTIMATED LIFE OF FINISH: less than 1 year

When it comes to exterior paints and stains, you absolutely do get what you pay for. Whatever brand or retailer you choose, buy its most premium product.

ABOVE: Recycled carriage house doors and windows left in their weather-beaten state serve as a visual reminder that a door opens into the lawn-mower garage. An office and spare bedroom are accessed from a more formal entrance on the side.

Extra wood and stain from this homeowner-built tool shed became stepping "stones" that get laid down during land scaping projects to protect the lawn.

LEFT: Wall shelves and tool hooks keep everything sorted and accessible so you can quickly grab what you need without creating an avalanche of things you don't.

FACING PAGE: When old tools are no longer usable, they get added to this outdoor display. Never store good tools outside, because the sun and rain will quickly age them.

POTTING SHED

It's amazing how much easier yard and household projects become when you have an organized arsenal of good tools and supplies at your fingertips.

around-the-shed plants

LEFT: Whether laying out annuals, perennials, or trees and shrubs, ignore the plants' current sizes and focus on how big they'll be when fully mature—information that's listed on the labels.

FACING PAGE: A lean-to tool closet has become so much a part of the landscape that plants have taken root on it.

A utility shed not only frees up space in your
garage so you can fit your car back inside, it
also puts your gear closer to where you use it.

ABOVE: Like an outdoor armoire, a reach-in tool rack puts everything from a watering can to a bulb planter right at eye level.

FACING PAGE: Part bicycle locker, part trellis, this unique shed wears walls of ivy.

garden
getaway

LEFT: Nestled deep in the corner of a vast property, this multipurpose structure provides a spot for doing everything from yoga to crafts projects to campouts.

ABOVE: Built-in shelving lines the walls and a wooden countertop rings the perimeter of the space.

working
sheds

RIGHT: Hang a wall shelf about 12 inches above your table, and you've got a great spot to stow supplies and completed work.

BELOW: Modular metal kitchen furniture is tough, waterproof, and available in whatever size and configuration you need to outfit your potting shed.

FACING PAGE: When a wall is unfinished, things can drop behind the shelving. If you will be storing items smaller than about 4 inches, install wallboard or plywood over the wall before hanging your shelves.

work surface tips

Putting a work surface in your shed will help with gardening, crafts, and other projects, says Seaside, California, professional organizer Cammie Jones (cjorganizing.com), who offers these design tips:

» Don't automatically make the surface the standard height of a table (30 inches) or kitchen countertop (36 inches). "People are all different sizes, and you don't want to be stooping over your work or reaching up to it," she says. "Put the surface a couple of inches below your elbows."

» Although you can use most any surface material for your worktable, Jones likes composite decking boards (such as Trex) because they're waterproof and durable.

» Despite all of the new storage options out there, you still can't beat pegboard for storing hand tools over your workbench.

photography credits

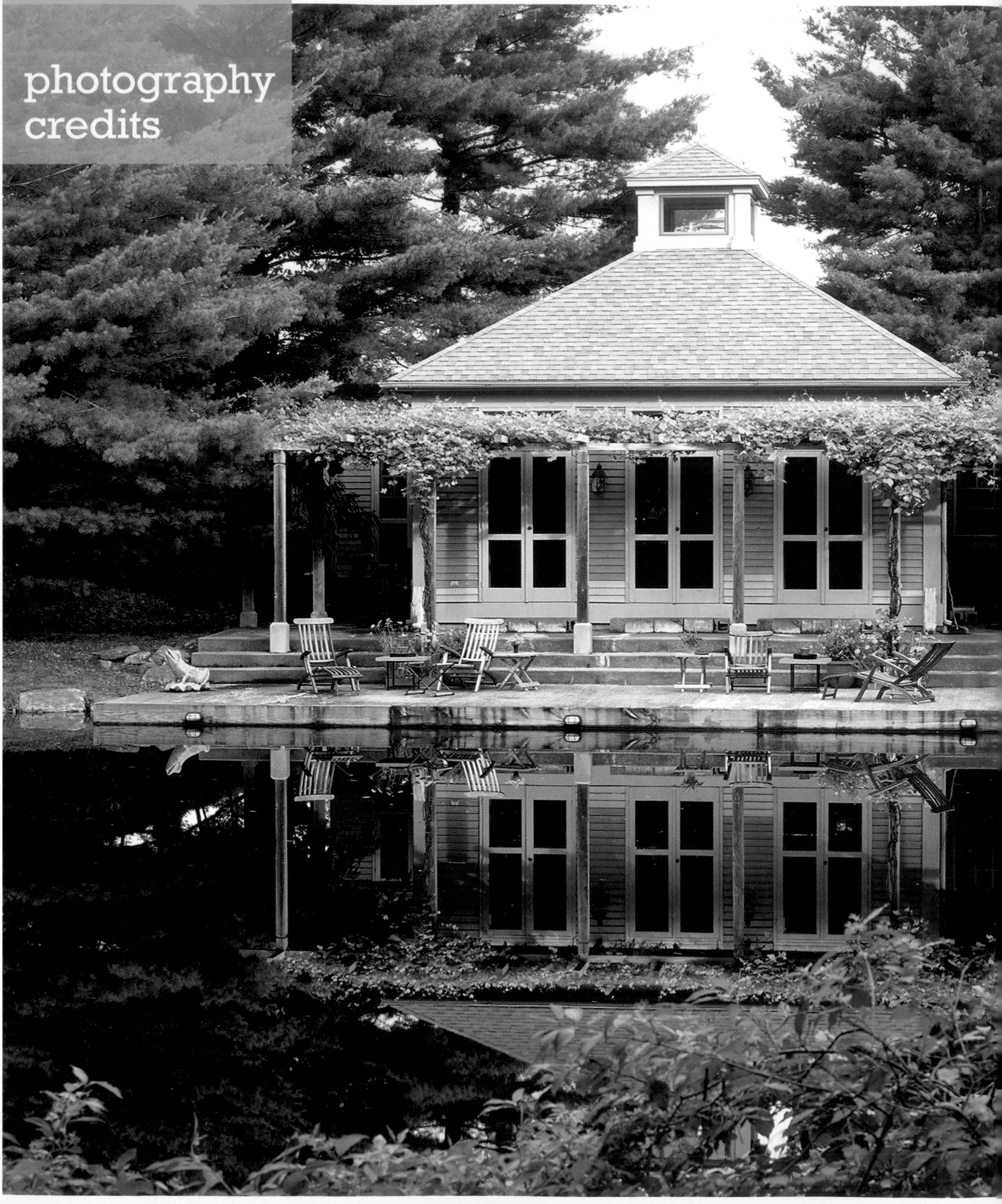